Gaza Alphabet

A - Z Guide to the Gaza that once was

Ashraf Hamad

First published in July 2024, Manchester, UK.

ISBN 978-1-0369-0635-1 (paperback)
ISBN 978-1-3999-9282-4 (ebook)

Self-Published by Ashraf Hamad

In loving memory of my dear father

Dr Mohammad Hamad

who died during the Gaza Genocide

31.10.1954

19.11.2024

"Silence for Gaza," by Mahmoud Darwish

Gaza is not the most beautiful city.
Its shore is not bluer than the shores of Arab cities.
Its oranges are not the most beautiful in the Mediterranean basin.

Gaza is not the richest city.

It is not the most elegant or the biggest, but it equals the history of an entire homeland, because it is more ugly, impoverished, miserable, and vicious in the eyes of enemies. Because it is the most capable, among us, of disturbing the enemy's mood and his comfort. Because it is his nightmare. Because it is mined oranges, children without a childhood, old men without old age and women without desires.

Because of all this it is the most beautiful, the purest and richest among us and the one most worthy of love.

Acknowledgments

This work would have been impossible to produce during the immense sadness and grief caused by the war on Gaza without the support of special people. I want to start by saying massive thank you to my always loving and always supportive wife, Dr Khawla Badwan. Thank you for being my critical friend who always believed in this project. I also wish to thank my wonderful children, Omar and Shams. You have been the light that kept me going as I bear witness to the unbearable while producing this guide.

To my dear friends Judith, Margaret, Patrick, Lena, and Alison thank you for being the first to listen to my ideas about this book. Your encouragement and belief in me provided the motivation I needed to keep going. Your support has been invaluable. I also want to acknowledge the illustrator who wished to remain anonymous. Your beautiful illustrations have offered a way to preserve the Gaza that we once knew.

Finally, this book is dedicated to Gaza and the people of Gaza. To the Gaza that once was and to the Gaza that is yet to become. This is a guide written with love in memory of all the love that the people of Gaza tried to establish against all the odds over many years. You are the true heroes who deserve a life of dignity and peace. Your resilience, struggle, and spirit are the inspiration behind every word written here.

Honouring Gaza

I have such a deep love for Gaza. I am familiar with its streets, camps, villages, and cities. My memories are filled with beautiful moments from my childhood and youth. The happiest times of my childhood were when my primary school organised trips around the Gaza Strip, from its southernmost point to the north. During these excursions, we visited historical landmarks, factories, amusement parks, and concluded the journey with delightful moments on Gaza's beach.

I have always wished for the entire world to have the opportunity to visit the Gaza Strip, spend time with its warm-hearted people, enjoy its mild climate, and experience the simplicity of life there. Unfortunately, political circumstances have continuously prevented this from happening.

In this guide, I aim to introduce the world to the Gaza I love, the city where I spent the best years of my life, the small piece of land that has made headlines worldwide. This guide is meant to commemorate a land and its people who have always dreamed of nothing but a dignified life, freedom, and justice.

Writing this book was a challenging journey, not because preparing the content was difficult or because sources were scarce, but because the memories I revisited while writing each page were filled with nostalgia and longing for beautiful days. They were also filled with grief over the loss of a city. I never imagined writing a book as a memorial to mourn Gaza. That said, the writing process gave me the determination to hold dear the memories of the Gaza that once stood. This book is about honouring Gaza and documenting some of its important landmarks. It is an act of struggle against the erasure of Gaza.

I hope you enjoy reading this book and that it provides you with a window into Gaza and the lives of its people. I hope it offers you more information about the city that millions around the world love but have not yet had the chance to visit.

Ashraf Hamad
UK, November 2024

This poem is in memory of **Dr Refaat Alareer**, inspired by his poetic masterpiece: *If I die.*

Gaza Alphabet is a flying kite over the Gaza that once was. A guide of tales, producing more tales.

A Kite

By Dr Khawla Badwan

Flying with the wind
Dancing in the air
About to fall
Trying not to fall
Rising above the ruins
Entangled with gazes
Fuelled with hope
Passing over a camp
A refugee camp
A death camp
A tent camp
With a tale
Telling tales
If you die
And I live
I'll fly the kite
Pass the tale
To a noisy world

The Phoenix of Gaza

Gaza, a small but special place along the eastern coast of the Mediterranean Sea. This narrow strip of land, stretching only 41 kilometres along the coast, is more than just a dot on the map; it is a vibrant place with a rich history and a resilient spirit, much like the mythical phoenix that symbolises renewal and revival.

Gaza's history is etched in gold, known for its fertile land and its central position in the ancient world. It has been called many names over the centuries: 'Hazati' by the Canaanites, 'Gazato' by the Egyptians, and 'Izzati' by the Assyrians. These names all reflect the city's strength and resilience. Today, it is often referred to as 'Ghazzat Hashem,' in honour of Hashem, the grandfather of Prophet Muhammad, who passed through Gaza during his travels.

Gaza has been a bustling crossroad of civilizations for thousands of years. Imagine merchants, travellers, and heroes from different eras passing through its land, each leaving a mark on its history. From the ancient Egyptians to the Greeks, and from the Romans to the Islamic Caliphates, Gaza has always been an important place where cultures met and stories began.

Today, Gaza is home to over 2.3 million people, making it one of the most densely populated areas in the world. Most of the people living there are Palestinian refugees and their descendants. The population is very young, with more than half of the people under the age of 18. They practice traditions in music, dance, cuisine, and embroidery that reflect their rich Palestinian heritage. The majority of Gazans are Sunni Muslims, but there is also a small, proud Christian community.

Gaza's geography is as diverse as its history. The land is generally flat, with sand dunes near the coast and fertile fields inland. This Mediterranean climate, with its mild, wet winters and hot, dry summers, allows farmers to grow a variety of crops like olives, citrus fruits, strawberries, and vegetables.

The economy of Gaza faces many difficulties due to blockades that restrict the movement of people and goods. These restrictions have led to high unemployment and poverty rates. However, the people of Gaza are incredibly resourceful and entrepreneurial, finding ways to start businesses and support their families despite these obstacles. The primary economic activities include agriculture, fishing, and small-scale manufacturing.

Living conditions in Gaza are tough. The blockade, which was imposed on the strip since 2006, has caused shortages of essential goods like medical supplies, fuel, and construction materials. The infrastructure needs a lot of repairs, and there are frequent power outages and limited access to clean water. Yet, the people of Gaza come together to support each other, showing a strong sense of community and solidarity.

Just like the phoenix, Gaza symbolises a cycle of renewal and revival. Despite facing many hardships, the spirit of Gaza and its people continues to rise from the metaphorical ashes, ready to face the future with hope, perseverance and determination.

And so, the story of Gaza continues, a tale of resilience and unity, where the heart of its people beats strong amidst the challenges, and their culture and traditions shine brightly for all the world to see.

A Al-Shifa Hospital

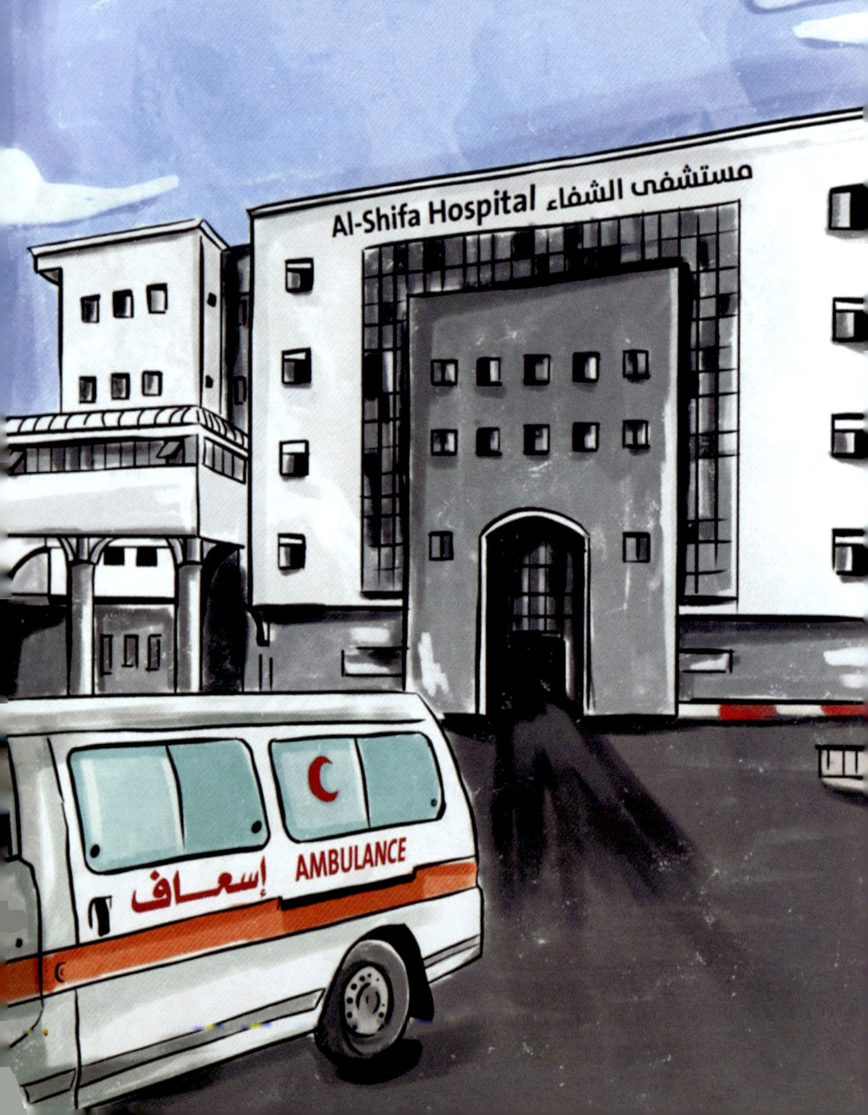

A *for* Al-Shifa Hospital

مُسْتَشْفَى الشِّفَاء

Al-Shifa Hospital is the largest medical institution providing services in the Gaza Strip. It was established in 1946 during the British Mandate. Initially, it consisted of small kiosks offering medical care to patients. Over time, it developed into a comprehensive medical complex that includes three specialised hospitals: the Surgery Hospital, the Internal Medicine Hospital, and the Women's and Maternity Hospital, along with many other specialised units. The hospital, covering an area of 45,000 square metres, is located at an intersection in the central western area of Gaza City. Al-Shifa Hospital serves the residents of Gaza City and also receives patients from other cities where specialised hospitals are not available.

B Barqouq Castle

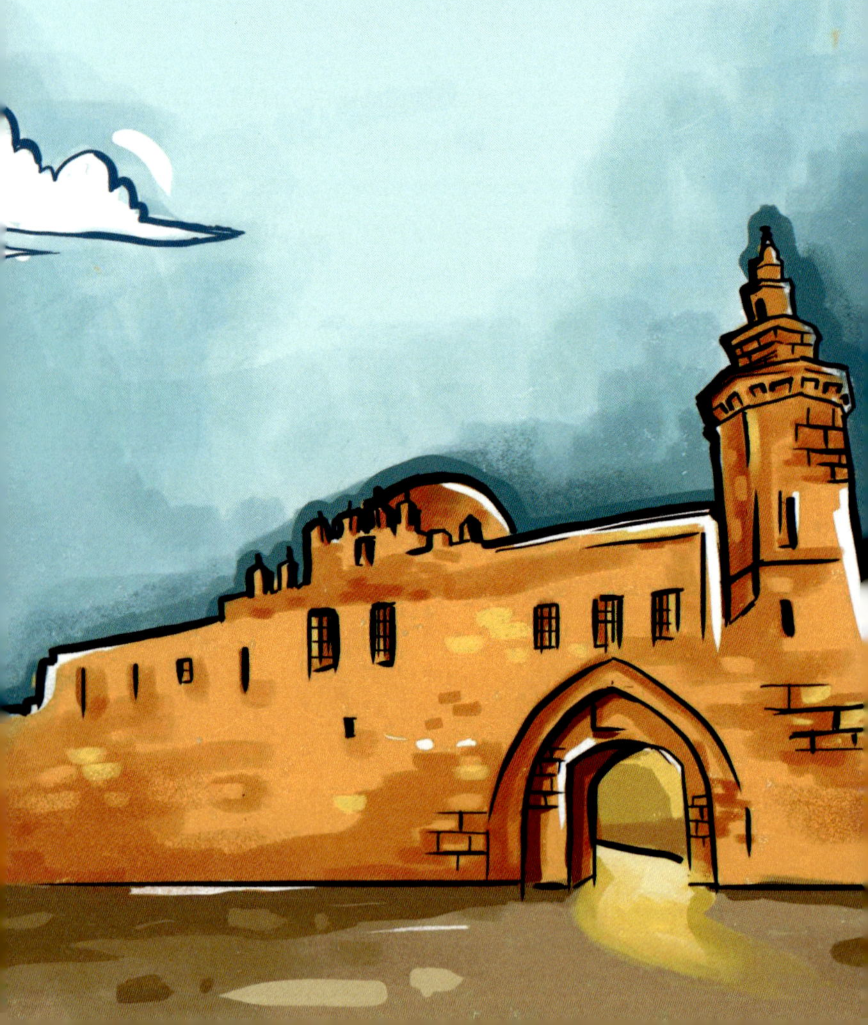

B *for* Barqouq Castle

قَلْعَة بَرْقُوق

If it's your first visit to Khan Younis, you should definitely check out Burqouq Castle. It's located right in the heart of the city. Take your time exploring the different parts of the castle; you can imagine the vibrant exchanges and stories that took place within its walls. It's like stepping back in time. Did you know that the castle dates back to 1387 AD? It was commissioned by Sultan Barqouq, a ruler of the Mamluk dynasty, and the construction was overseen by Prince Younis Bin Abdullah Al-Noorozi. It was originally designed to safeguard the city, but it wasn't just for defense. The castle also served as a gathering place for merchants and travelers on their way to the major Mamluk capitals of the era, Cairo and Damascus.

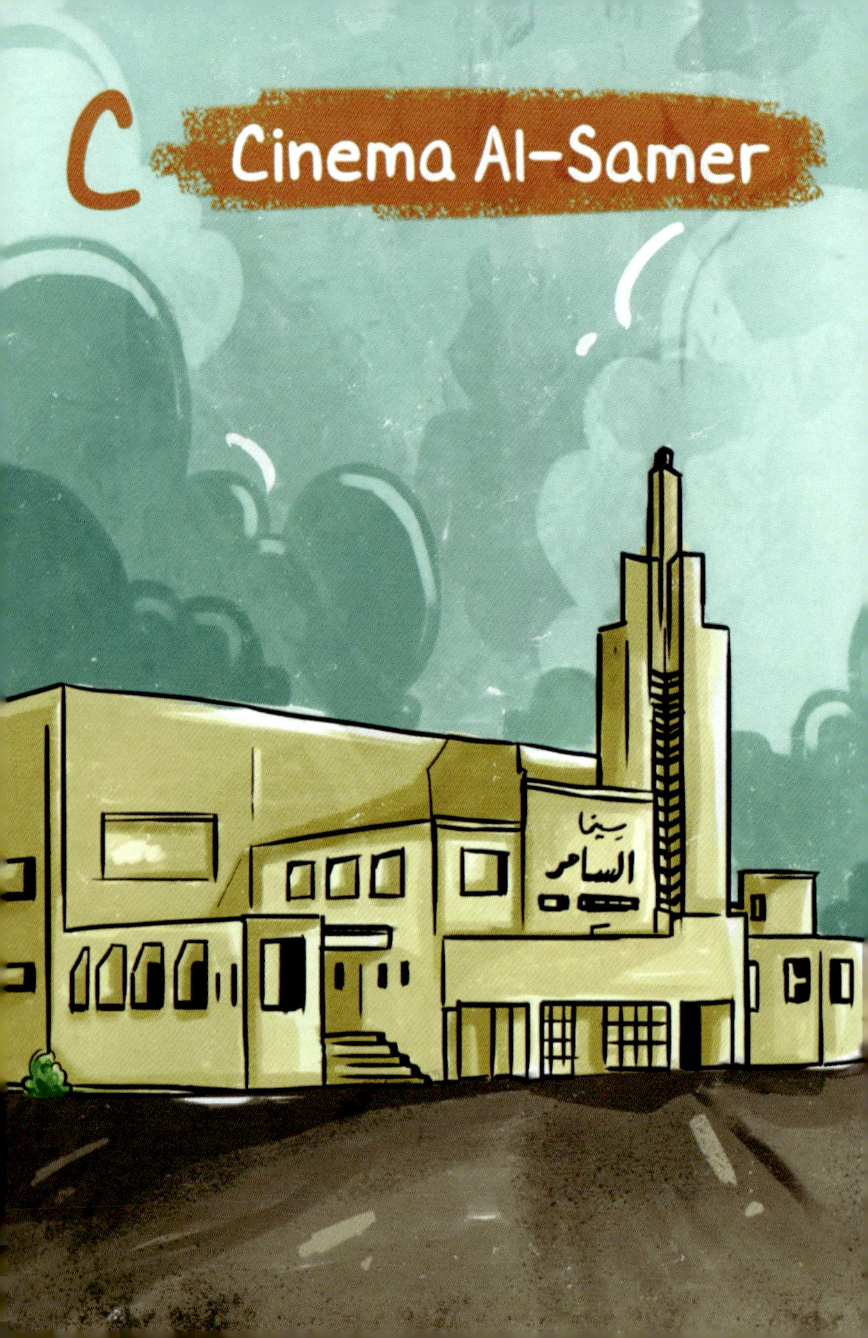
C
Cinema Al-Samer
سينما
السامر

C *for* Cinema Al-Samer

سِينَمَا السَّامِر

You may wonder, is there a movie theater in Gaza? Yes, there once was. Established by Rashad Al-Shawa in 1944 as Gaza's first cinema, Cinema Al-Samer was closed more often than it was open. The residents of Gaza longed to see Egyptian, Indian, and Western films there, but the circumstances and challenges during the 1987 Intifada, coupled with security restrictions and curfews imposed by the Israeli occupation, turned this cinema into a closed landmark. Efforts to revive Cinema Al-Samer over the past two decades have not succeeded, leading the people of Gaza to focus on producing films that travel the world and tell their own stories, rather than importing films that do not reflect their reality. Despite its closure, Cinema Al-Samer remains a significant landmark in the Gaza Strip, serving as a familiar reference point for locals navigating the area.

D Dabkeh

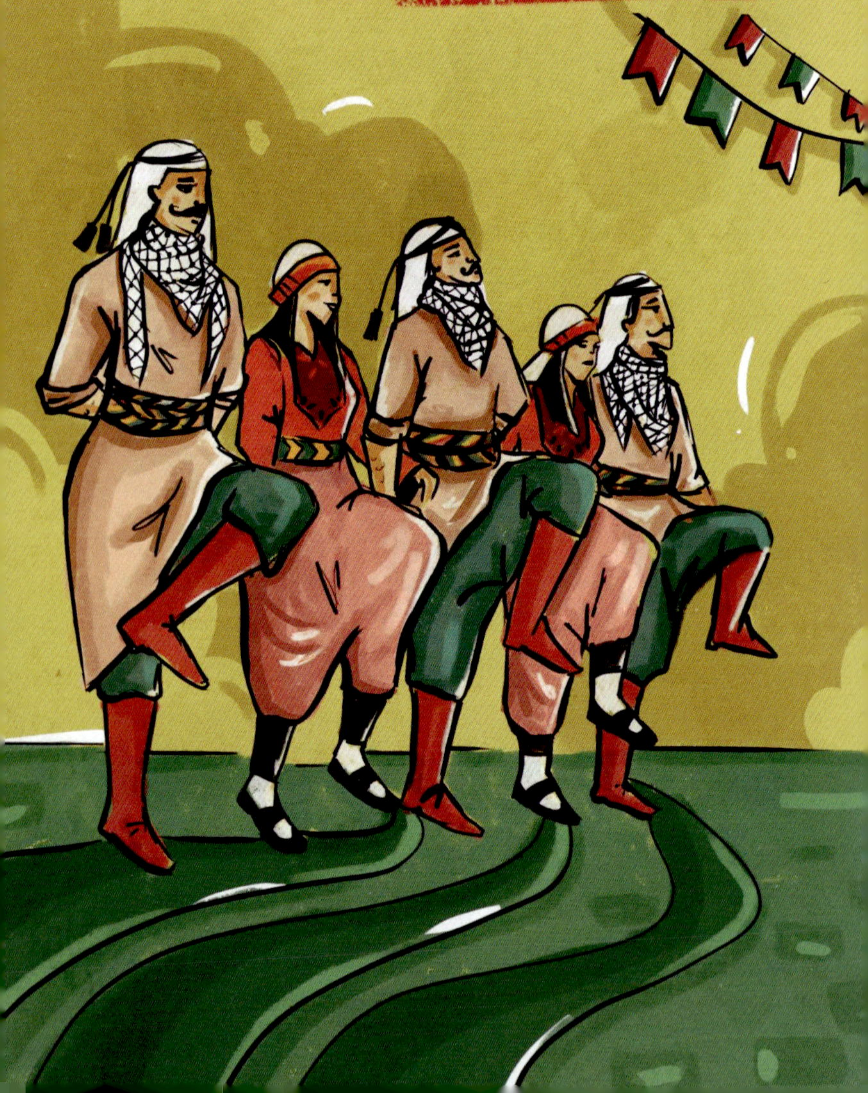

D *for* Dabkeh

دَبْكِة

Once you try it, you'll agree that Dabkeh truly captures the spirit and resilience of the people of Gaza. It's more than just a dance for us; it's a treasured tradition passed down through generations. Dabkeh involves dancers linking hands, symbolising unity and solidarity. The stomping steps display not only strength but also a deep connection to our land. Dabkeh is a staple at Palestinian weddings, and its vibrant energy fills nearly every celebration. In recent years, Dabkeh has transcended its local roots to become a powerful symbol of Palestinian identity. Through Dabkeh, we proudly share our rich heritage with the world.

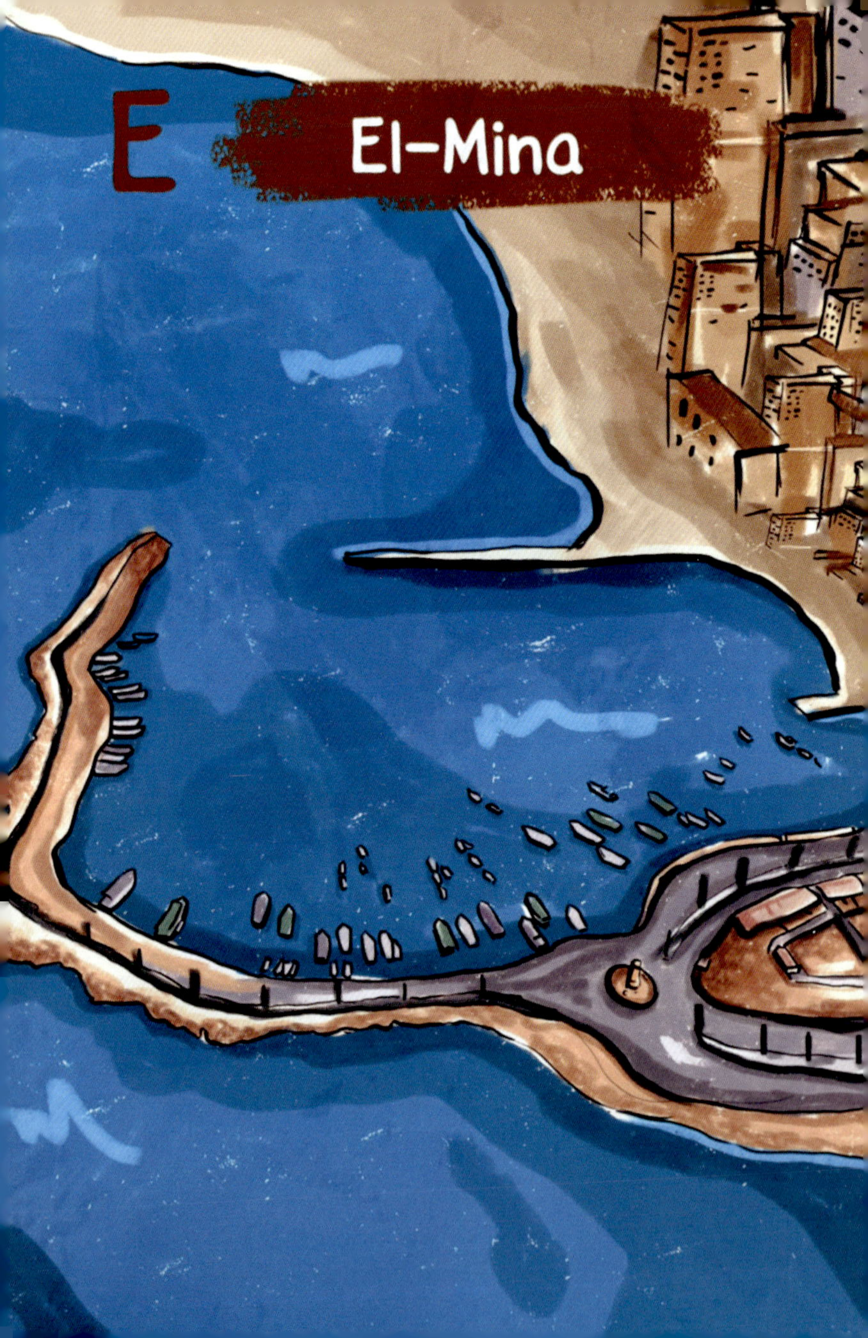
E
El-Mina

E for El-Mina

المَيناء

Some argue that sunset is the best time to visit, while others believe you should spend an entire day at El-Mina, the harbour of Gaza City, to enjoy an unforgettable and exciting experience. El-Mina is a vibrant and bustling hub that plays a crucial role in the lives and livelihoods of Gazans. Nestled along the picturesque Mediterranean coast, this harbour is essential for trade and fishing, providing income for many locals. The sight of colourful fishing boats docked along the shore is iconic, reflecting the rich maritime heritage of the region. Historically significant, El-Mina has been mentioned in ancient texts and was a central point in trade routes. Visitors can explore the fresh seafood markets, enjoy the stunning coastal views, and witness the enduring spirit of Gaza. The harbour area also serves as a local tourist spot, where families relax, enjoy snacks and ice cream from vendors at sunset.

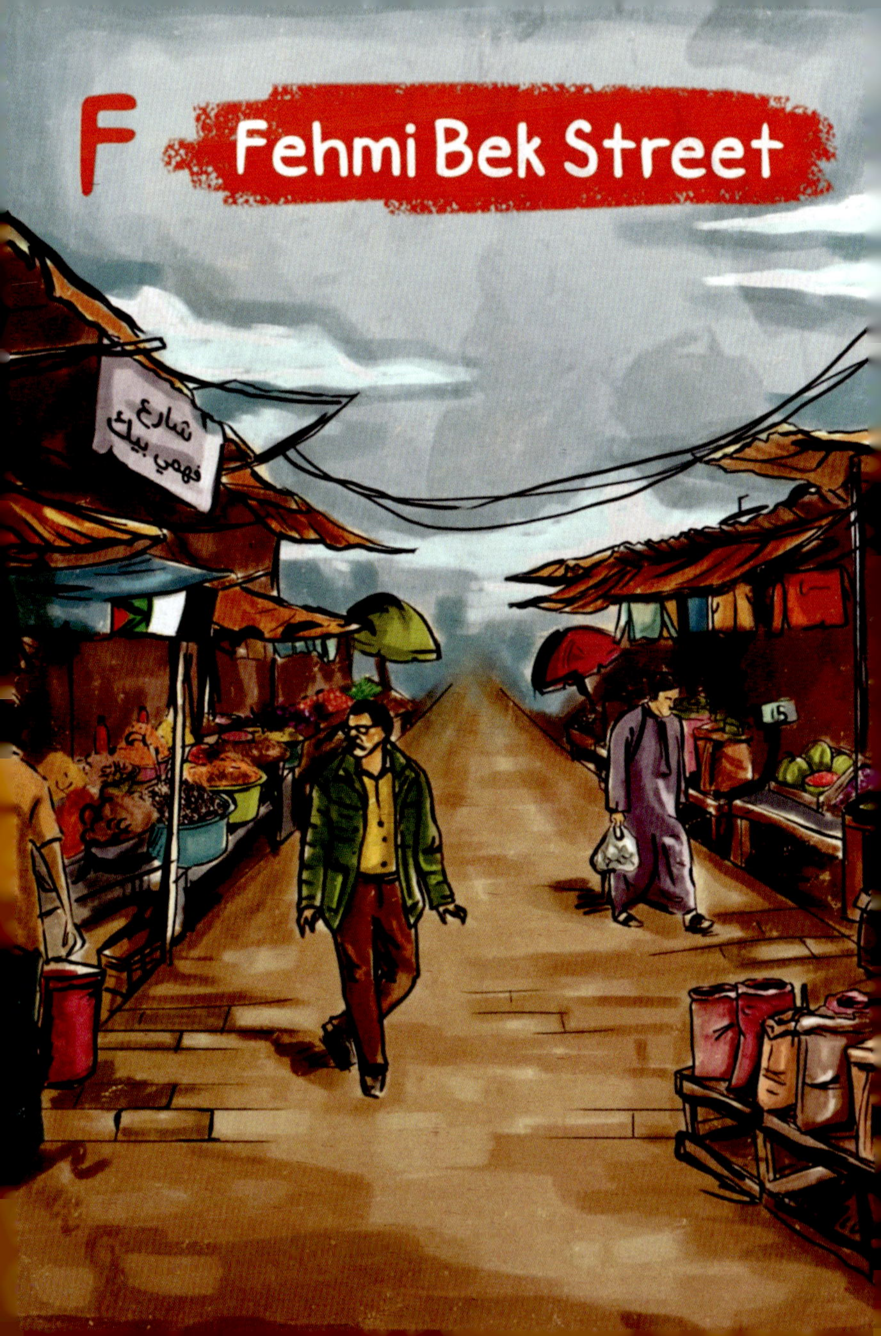
F
Fehmi Bek Street
شارع
فهمي بيك
15

F *for* Fehmi Bek Street

شَارِع فِهْمِي بِيك

So, you know, it's a very busy area. Take your time and enjoy it. Fehmi Bek Street is right in the centre of Old Town of Gaza City and is a bustling spot for travelers and shoppers moving from Rafah in the south to Beit Hanoun in the north. Connecting Omar Al-Mukhtar Street and Palestine Square to the south with Al-Wehda Street to the north, Fehmi Bek Street is quite compact, just 200 meters long and 10 meters wide, but it's packed with history and activity. The street is rich with stories from Gaza's Ottoman past. It's a lively area named after Fehmi Bek Al-Husseini, Gaza's first mayor who was elected in 1928 during the British Mandate.

G 'Gaza Welcomes You' sign

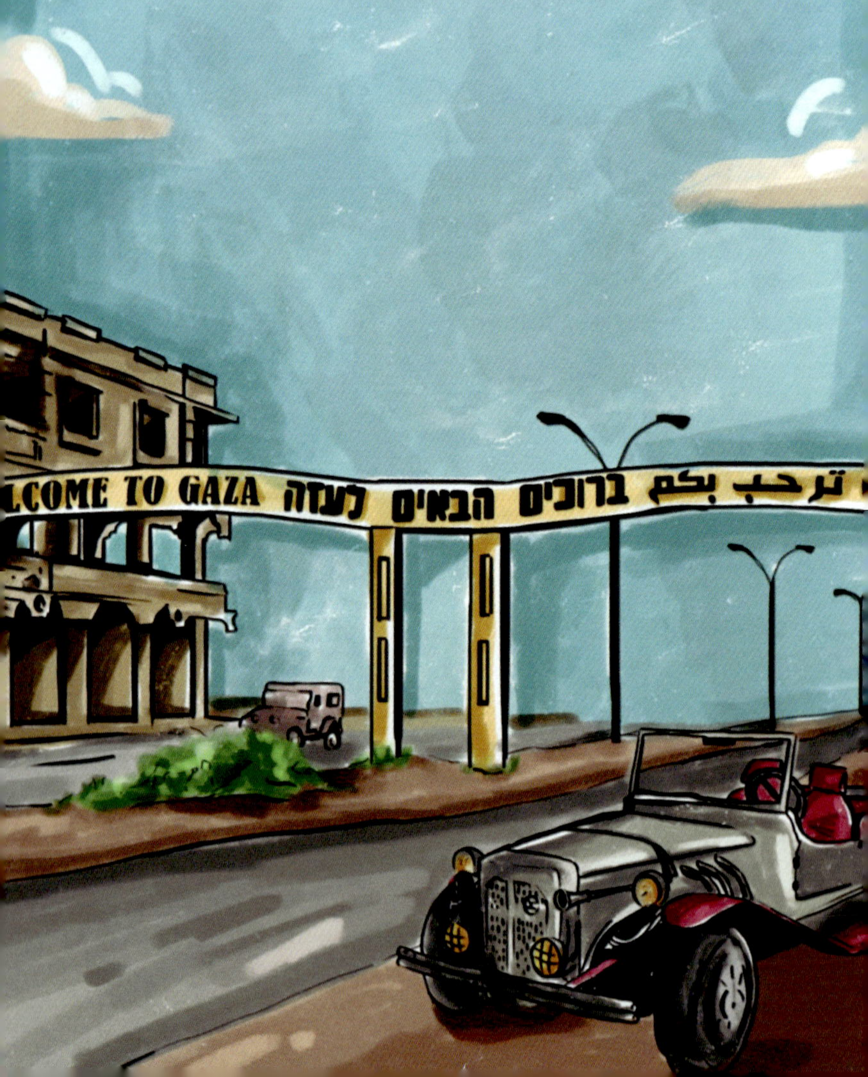

G *for* 'Gaza Welcomes You' sign

غَزَّة تُرَحِبُ بِكُم

You can ask your local driver to drop you off near the "Gaza Welcomes You" sign on Salah Al-Din Street in the Zeitoun neighbourhood. Locals often use this landmark as a convenient reference point for giving directions and locating addresses. The sign has been around for a long time, though we're not exactly sure when it was first installed. Photographs from the 1970s show the sign displaying "Gaza Welcomes You" in Arabic, English, and Hebrew. Now it only presents the greeting in Arabic and English.

H Hashem Mosque

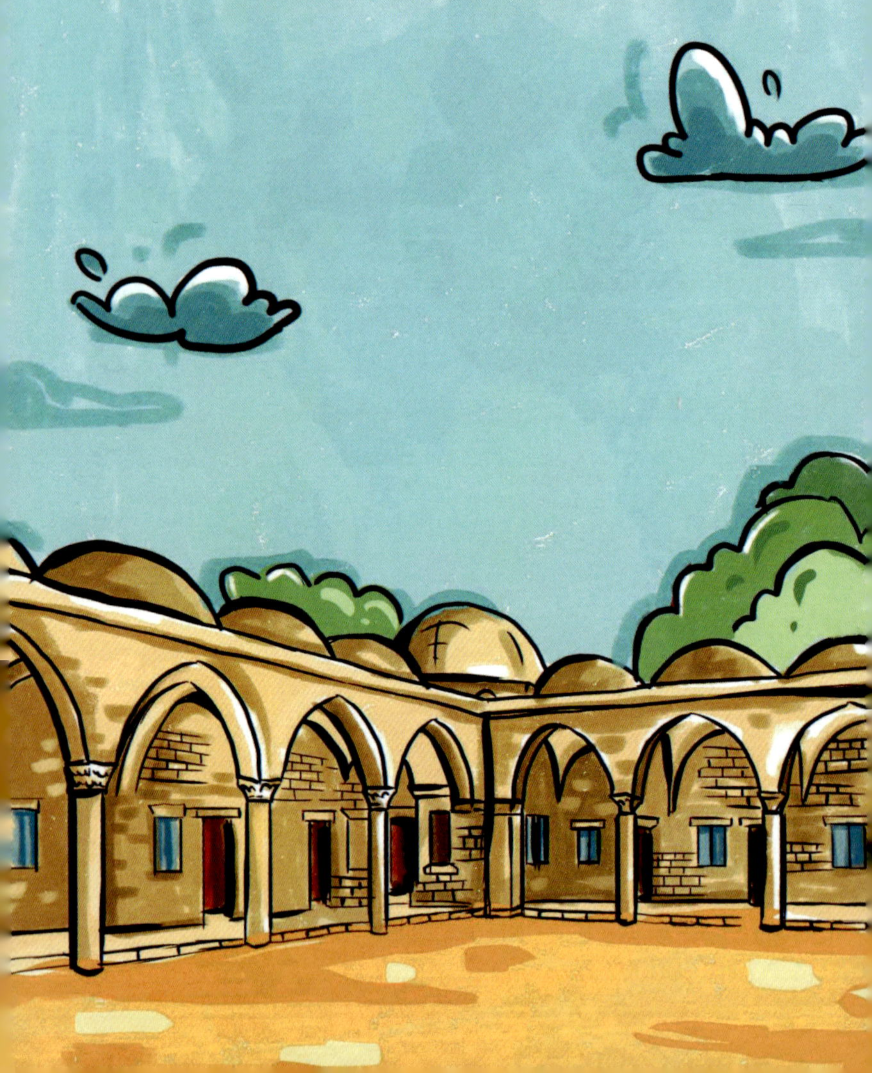

H *for* Hashem Mosque

مَسْجِدُ هَاشِم

It's a must-visit place. Set aside a couple of hours to enjoy a visit to Sayed Hashim Mosque in the Old Town of Gaza City. The mosque is famous for housing the grave of the Prophet Muhammad's great-grandfather, Hashim bin Abd Manaf. Originally built by the Mamluks, it was later refurbished by Ottoman Sultan Abdul Majid in 1850. Although it was damaged during World War I, it was restored by the Supreme Islamic Council in Palestine. Today, the mosque serves as a central spiritual, cultural, and educational hub in the neighbourhood.

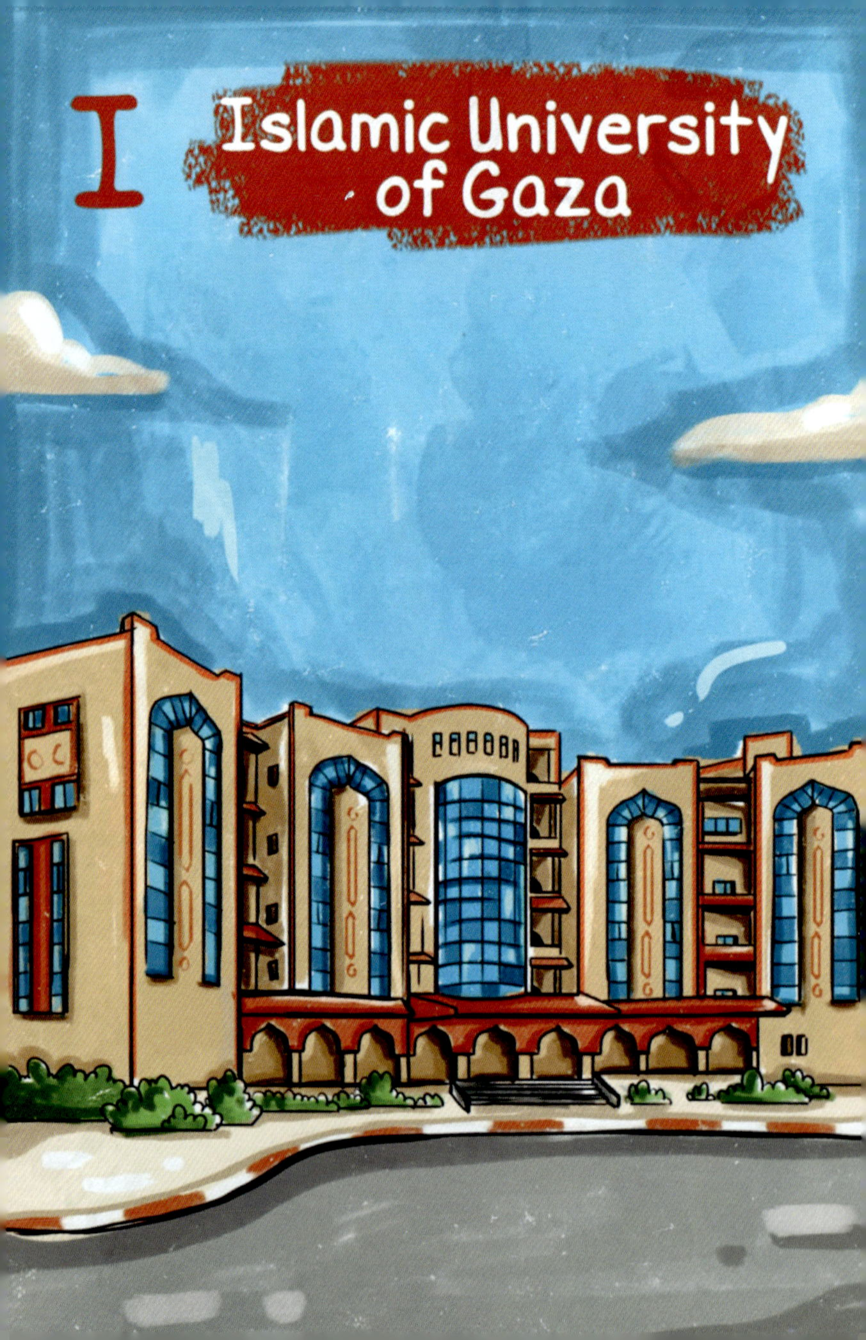
I
Islamic University
of Gaza

I *for* Islamic University of Gaza

الجَامِعَة الإِسْلَامِيَّة فِي غَزَّة

Whether you're interested in a campus tour or visiting its library, the Islamic University of Gaza (IUG), the largest academic institution in the Gaza Strip, will offer you a great experience. Established in 1978 with only five staff members and 25 students, the university began with three colleges that were foundational in providing essential education to the community. Over the years, the university's vision expanded, adding more colleges, programmes, staff, and students. Today, it is one of the largest universities in the occupied Palestinian territories. The main campus is in the heart of Gaza City. This vibrant area is home to many governmental and academic institutions, such as Al-Azhar University, Al-Aqsa University, and the headquarters of the UNRWA.

J Al-Jondi Al-Majhoul

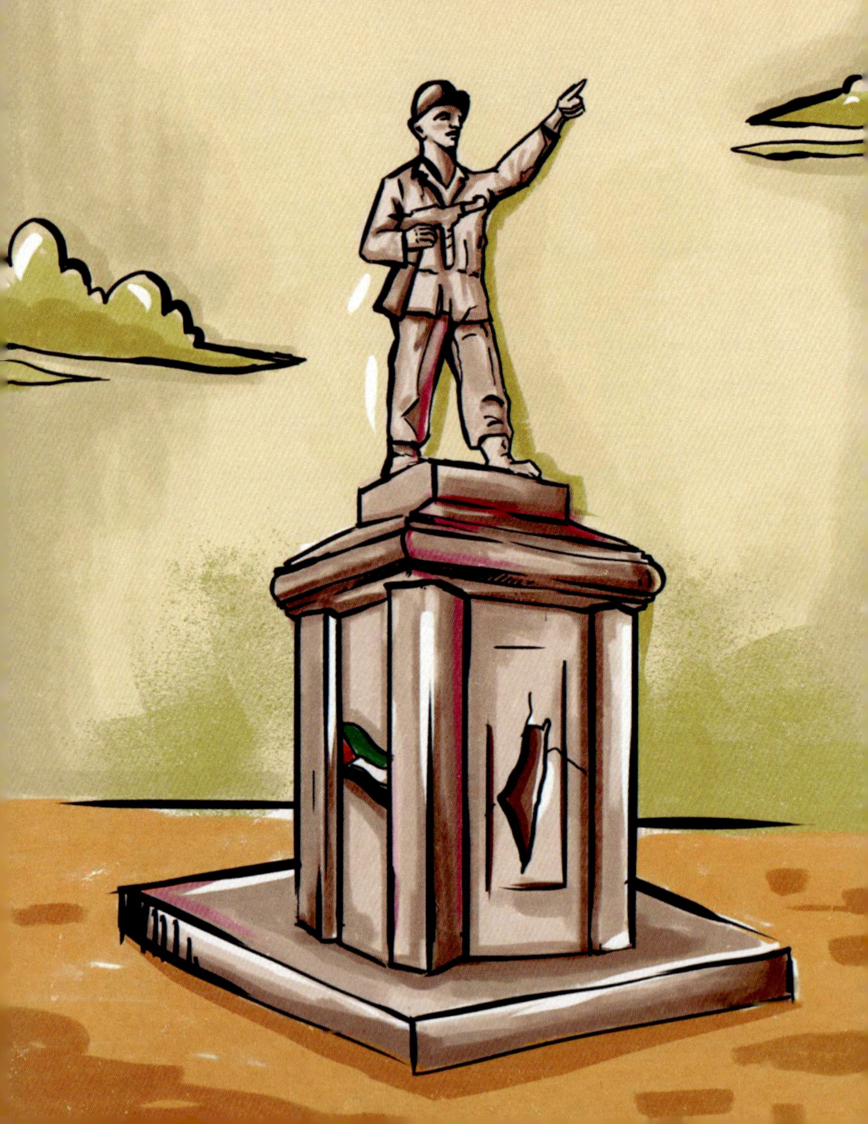

J *for* Al-Jondi Al-Majhoul

الجُنْدِي المَجْهُول

On your way from the Old Town of Gaza to Gaza Beach, be sure to pass by the Al-Jundi Al-Majhoul (The Unknown Soldier) Monument. You can't miss it. It stands in the park directly across from the Palestinian Legislative Council building on Omar Al-Mukhtar Street, in the heart of Gaza City. The monument, a significant landmark, was established in 1957, destroyed in 1967, and rebuilt in 2000. It's a powerful symbol for the people of Gaza, often serving as a backdrop for numerous national events and demonstrations, embodying the resilience and spirit of the people. The structure features a two-meter-tall marble base, and at the top, there is a statue of a soldier in full combat attire, holding a weapon in his right hand and pointing towards Jerusalem (Al-Quds) with his left index finger.

K Knafah

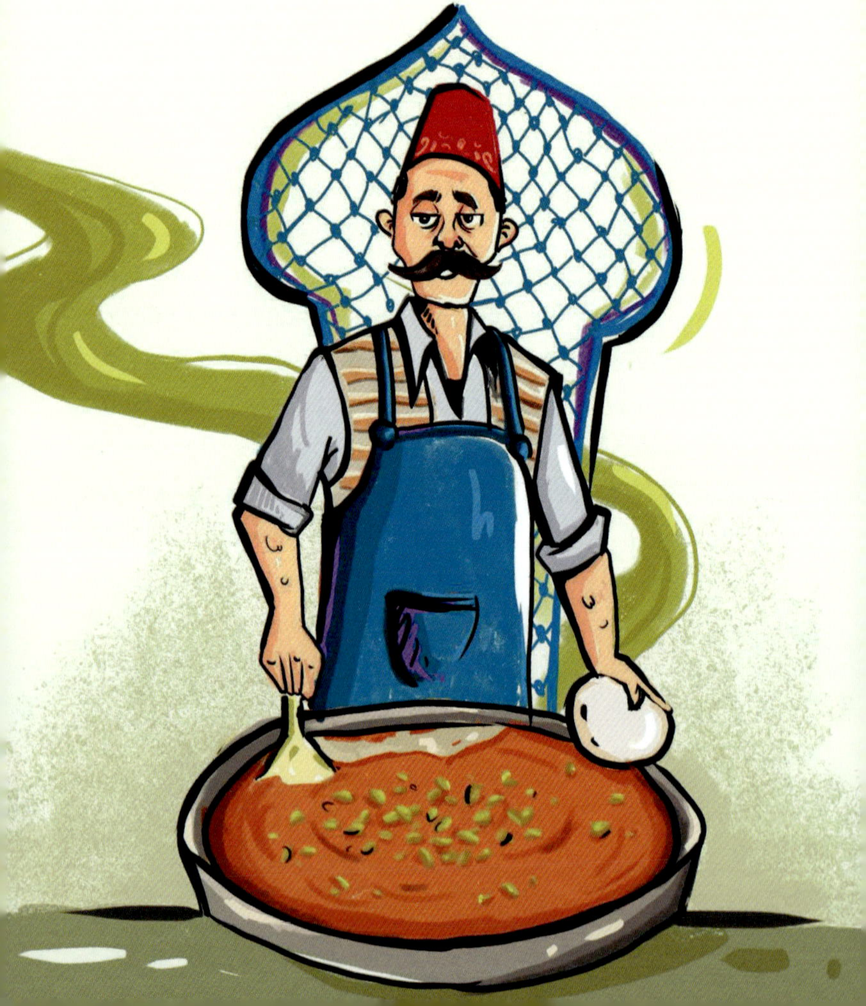

K *for* Knafah

كنافة

If you make it to Gaza, you should definitely try Knafah at least once. This traditional dessert is popular all over Palestine and comes in many varieties and flavours, making it hard to choose between. My advice is to try them all! Start with Knafah Arabia, also known as Gaza-style Knafah. It's slightly salty and rich, flavoured with a unique blend of nuts, nutmeg, and cinnamon. You should also try the renowned Knafah Nabulsiya, made with layers of specially prepared shredded dough and unsalted cheese, topped with a sprinkle of ground pistachios and drizzled with thick syrup. One more tip: enjoy your Knafah with Gazan coffee flavoured with cardamom.

L

Louz

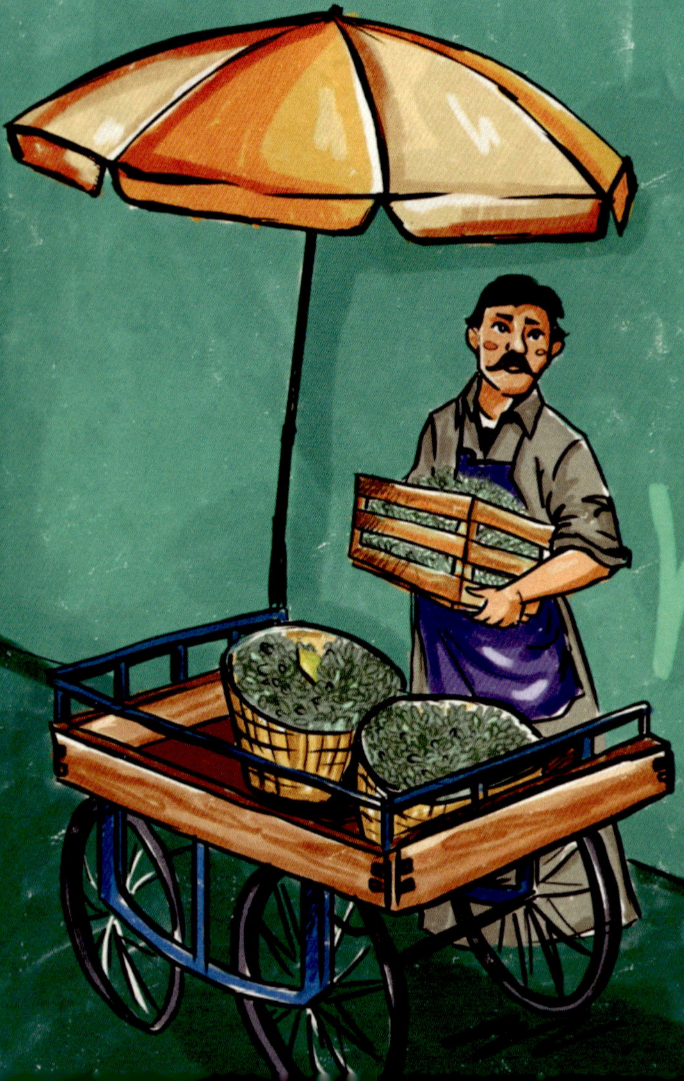

L *for* Louz

لـُوز

They're a real treat around here; Louz (green almonds) signals the start of spring in Palestine. Louz has a unique taste that combines both sweet and bitter flavours. Palestinians love eating them fresh and green. Louz trees are commonly found along the eastern borders of the Gaza Strip, especially in the central and southern regions. They thrive with little care and mainly depend on rainfall. Walking through Gaza's streets in March, you'll see roadside and local markets bustling with vendors selling these cherished green almonds. You can eat them fresh and raw, or if you want to experience them the way Gazans do, dip the Louz in a bit of salt to enhance the flavour. Give it a try and see what you like best.

M Maqloubeh

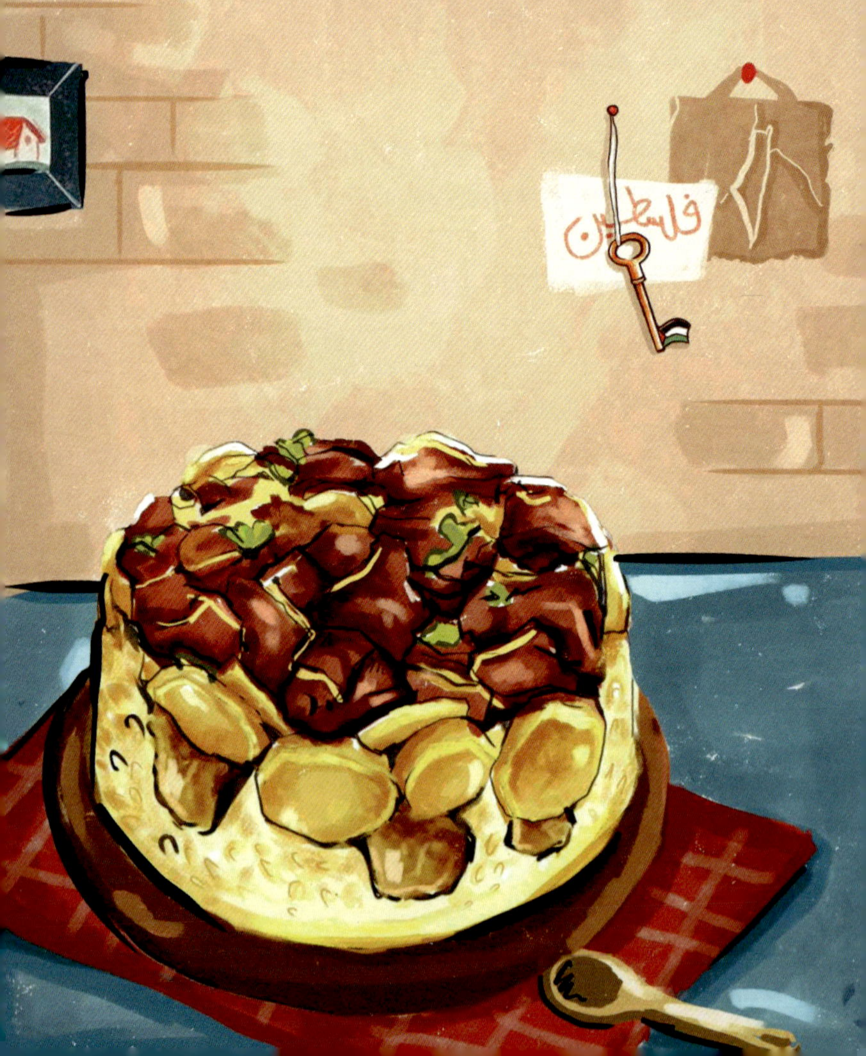

M *for* Maqloubeh

مَقْلُوبَة

I can't recommend enough having Maqluba in a Palestinian home. If you get the chance, join a family meal and enjoy the authentic flavours and hospitality. Maqloubeh is a dish with deep roots in Palestine, cherished since ancient times. It was originally known as "Baathenjaniya" because the main ingredient is "baathenjan," or aubergine. The name Maqloubeh means "upside down" and refers to the way it's served. The cooking process involves placing meat or chicken and various vegetables at the bottom of the pot, then adding rice on top. When it's ready, the pot is flipped over so that the rice ends up on the bottom, with the meat and vegetables on top. Maqloubeh has become internationally recognised as a symbol of Palestinian endurance. It's not just a dish; it represents our culture and resilience.

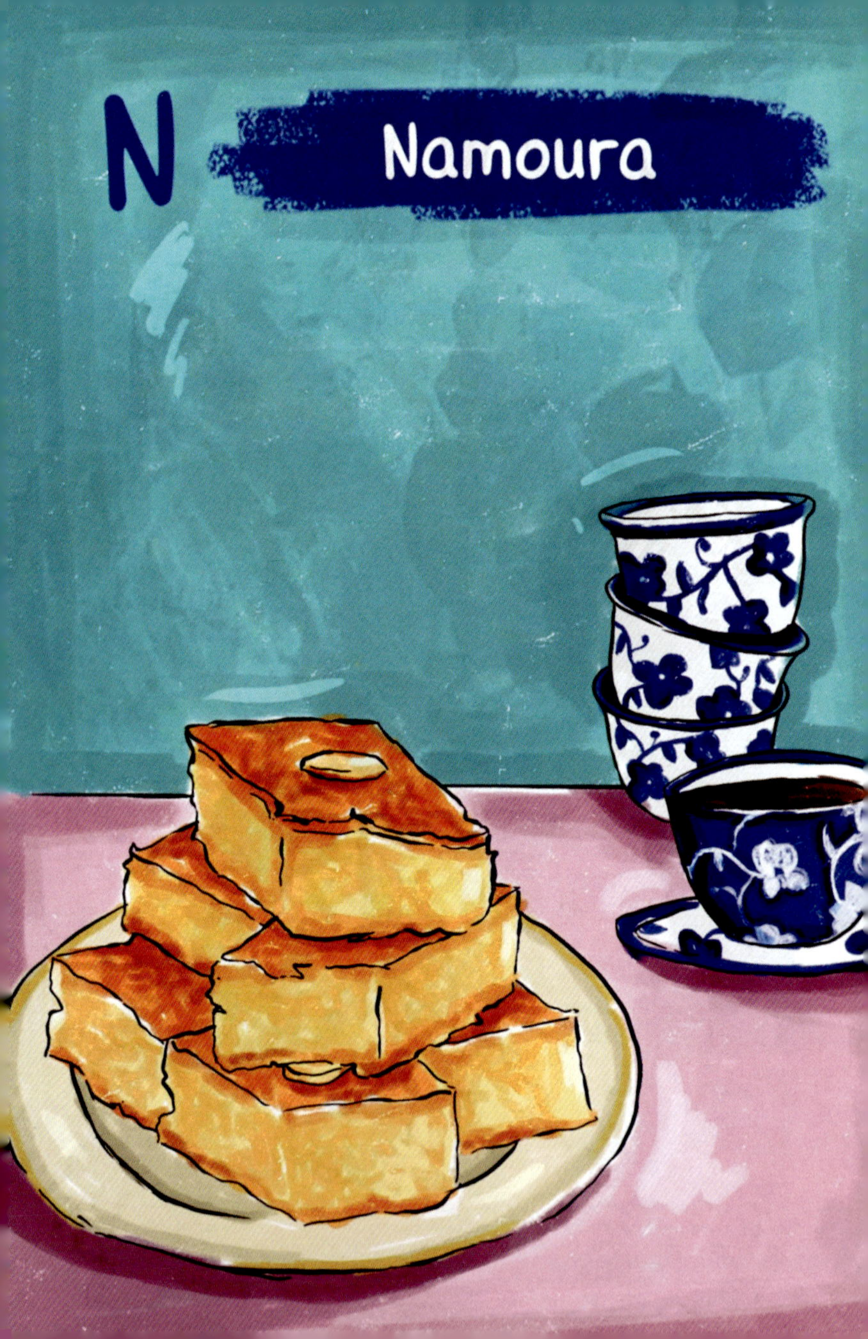
N
Namoura

N *for* Namoura

نَمُورَة

If you visit Gaza during the winter months, you should try Namoura. It's one of the most popular desserts in the Gaza Strip. It's delicious and affordable, making it a favourite among locals. Namoura is packed with energy, being high in sugar, fat, and the vitamins found in nuts. Gazans typically enjoy Namoura during joyous occasions like weddings, graduations, and social visits. For many years, Namoura has also been a common gift that Gazans bring to their relatives and friends outside the Gaza Strip. It's a way to share a taste of home. I recommend trying it fresh from a local sweet shop.

O Al-Omari Mosque

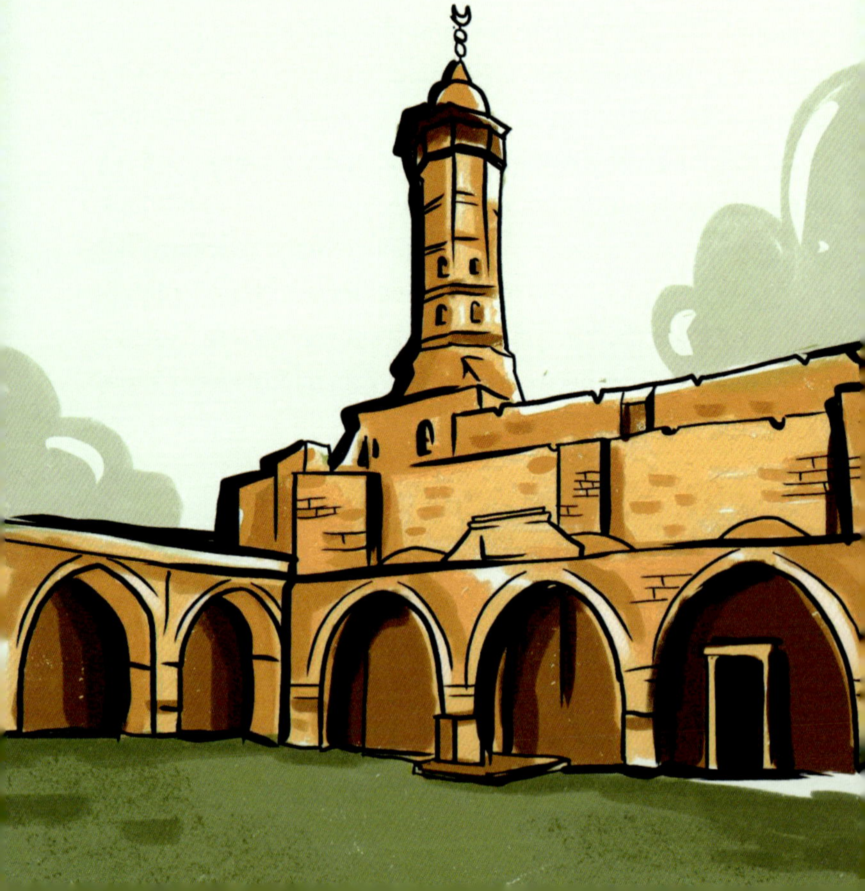

O *for* Al-Omari Mosque

المَسْجِد العُمَرِي

If you enjoy historical places, then the Al-Omari Mosque is a must-visit. It is one of the oldest and most historic mosques in the Gaza Strip. A bit of history: it was established during the caliphate of Omar Ibn Al-Khattab. Originally a Roman-era temple, it was later converted into a church, and after the Islamic conquest, it became Gaza's largest mosque. The mosque is situated in the heart of the Old Town of Gaza City, in the Al-Daraj neighbourhood. Walking towards the mosque, you can see its minaret from afar. I recommend taking your time exploring the mosque and its surroundings. The nearby Qaysariyya Market (Gold Market) and Al-Zawiya Market are also worth a visit.

P

Church of Saint Porphyrius

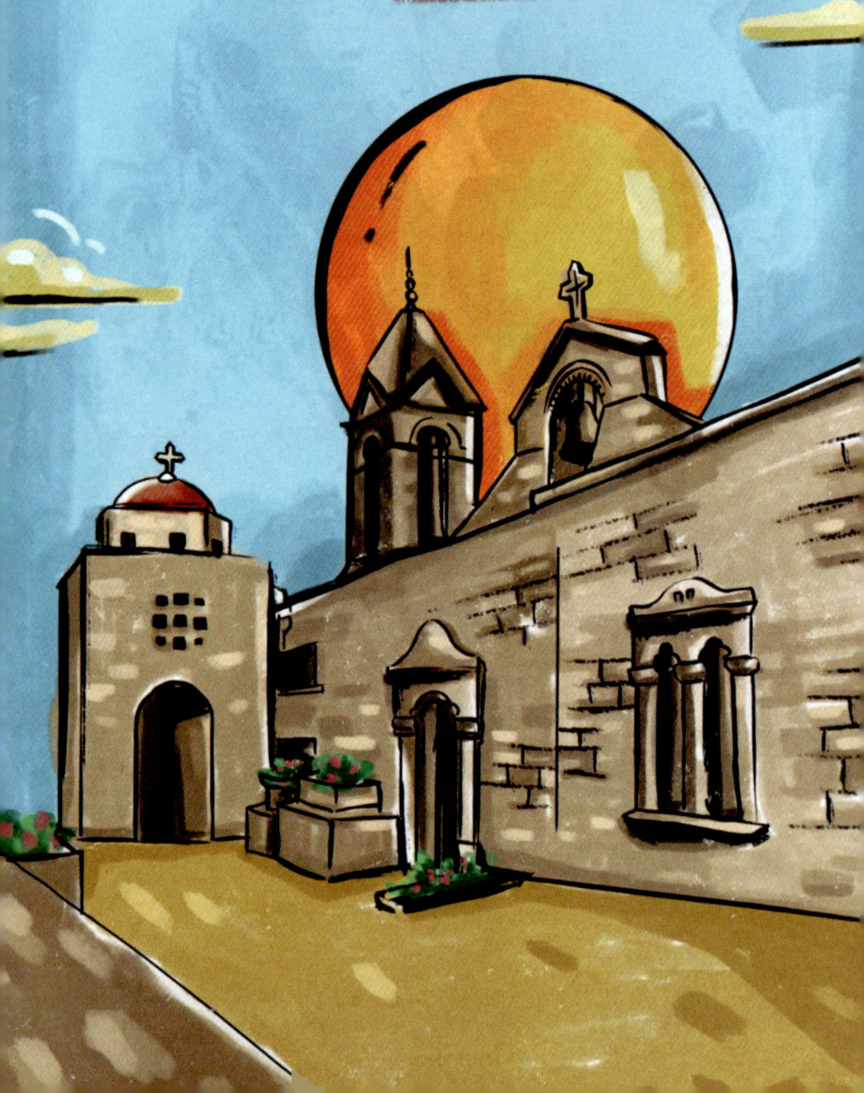

P *for* Church of Saint Porphyrius

كَنيسَة القِديس بُرفِيرْيُوس

A short walk from Al-Omari Mosque takes you to Saint Porphyrius Church, one of the oldest churches in the world. Locally, Gazans call it the "Greek Orthodox Church". The church was initially built in 425 AD, renovated in 1856, and most recently restored in 2020. You'll be captivated by the church's beautiful Byzantine-inspired design, featuring marble columns with Corinthian carvings and lotus flowers. I recommend visiting during a service if you can—it's a unique experience. Don't hesitate to talk to the locals; they often have fascinating stories about the church's history.

Q

Qasr Al-Pasha

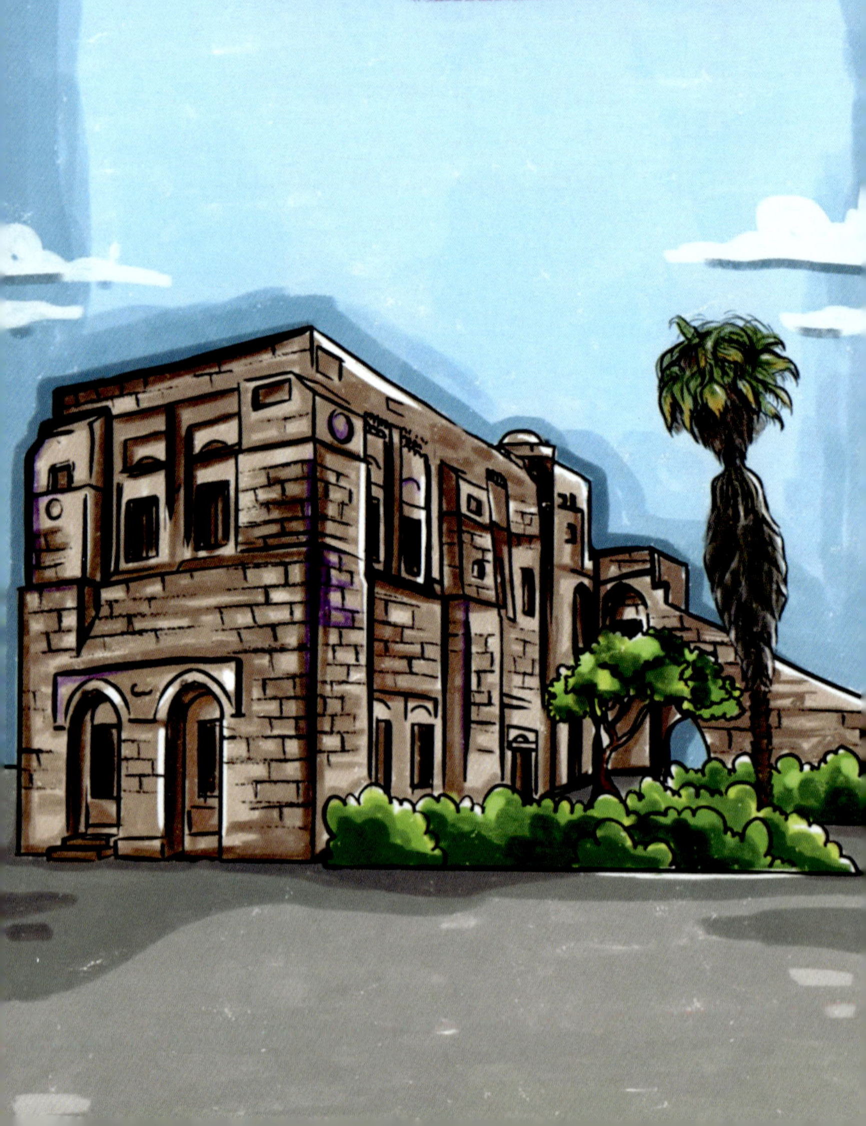

Q *for* Qasr Al-Pasha

قَصْرُ البَاشَا

Don't be intimidated by the symbol of the two facing lions at the entrance of Qasr Al-Pasha (the Lord's Palace). These lions are said to represent the Muslims' victory over the Mongols and Crusaders. Qasr Al-Pasha is located in the Al-Daraj neighbourhood of the Old Town in Gaza City. It's a fascinating two-storey building that dates back to the era of Mamluk Sultan Al-Zahir Rukn Al-Din Baybars. The palace served as the residence for the rulers of Gaza during the Mamluk and Ottoman eras. It has a rich history and was a significant administrative centre. When you visit, you'll notice that the palace has been converted into a museum. Inside, five rooms are dedicated to displaying archaeological artifacts, including coins, pottery, copper jugs, and bronze and iron pieces. These artifacts date back to the Greek, Roman, Byzantine, and Islamic periods.

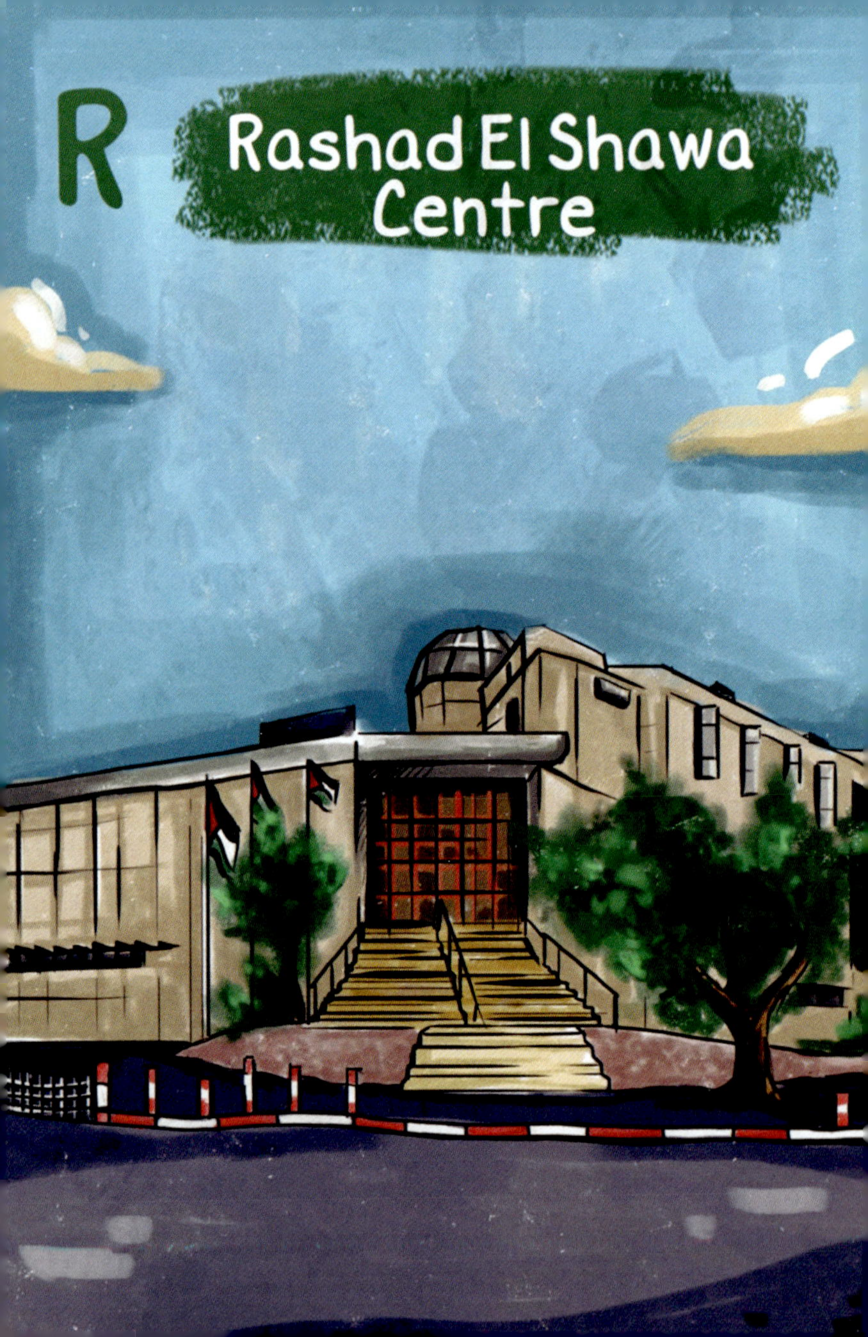
R
Rashad El Shawa
Centre

R *for* Rashad El Shawa Centre

مَرْكَزُ رَشَاد الشَّوَّا

Whether you're interested in attending art exhibitions, intellectual seminars, plays, or international conferences, you should consider visiting the Rashad El Shawa Cultural Centre. Established in 1988 by Rashad El Shawa, who served as the Mayor of Gaza for 11 years, it is the first cultural centre in Palestine. The centre plays a crucial role in enriching the cultural life of the Gaza Strip. Located in a well-known spot in Gaza City, it is close to key institutions like Al-Shifa Hospital and the Palestinian Legislative Council headquarters, making it a convenient reference point for many. Whether you visit on a weekday or a weekend, there's always something interesting happening. A final tip: make sure to visit the public library hosted by the centre.

S Al-Samrah Bath

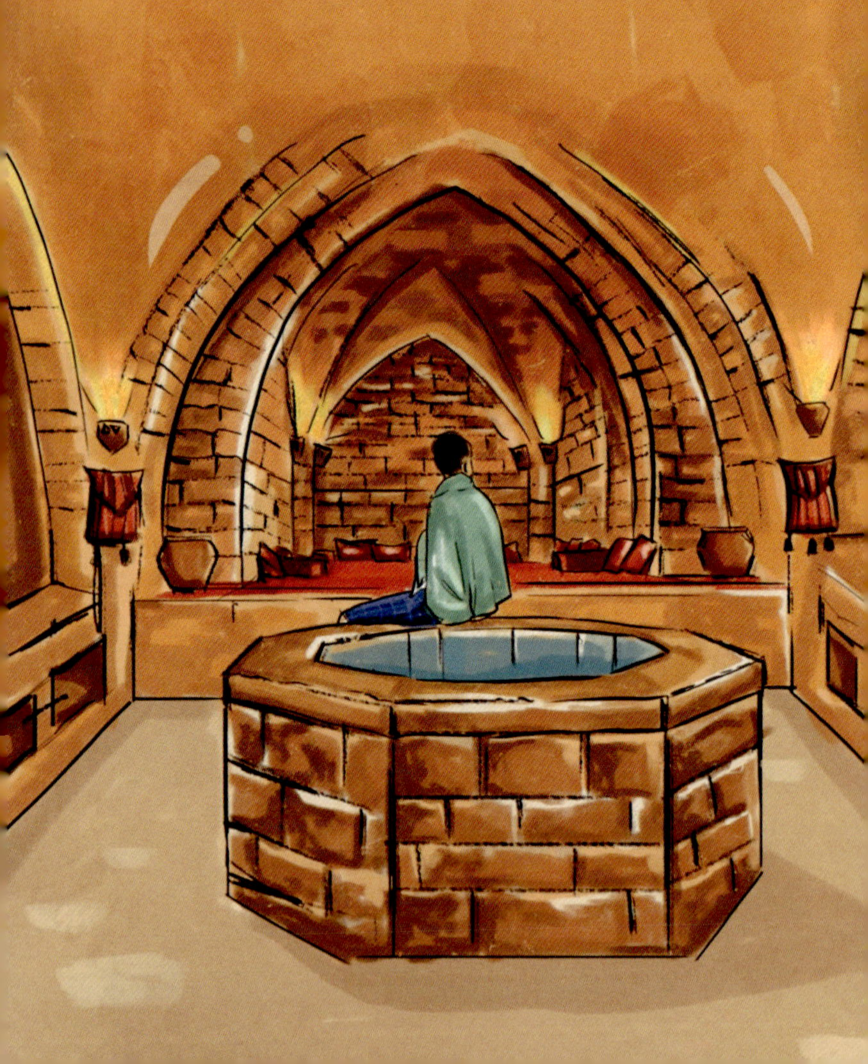

S *for* Al-Samrah Bath

حَمَّامُ السَّمْرَة

Be sure to experience this piece of history for yourself. It's more than just a bath, Al-Samrah Bath is a journey through time and tradition, offering both relaxation and a glimpse into Gaza's rich heritage. This bathhouse, the last of its kind from the Ottoman era, was built and restored over 865 years ago. Its name, Hammam Al-Samra, comes from the Samaritan Jews who once worked here. Located in the Al-Zaytoun neighbourhood, the bathhouse is designed to guide you through a gradual transition from a hot room to a warm room, and finally to a cold room. This unique design makes it a favourite among Gazans, both men and women, especially during the winter months. They come here to enjoy a warm bath and boost their circulation.

T Tatreez

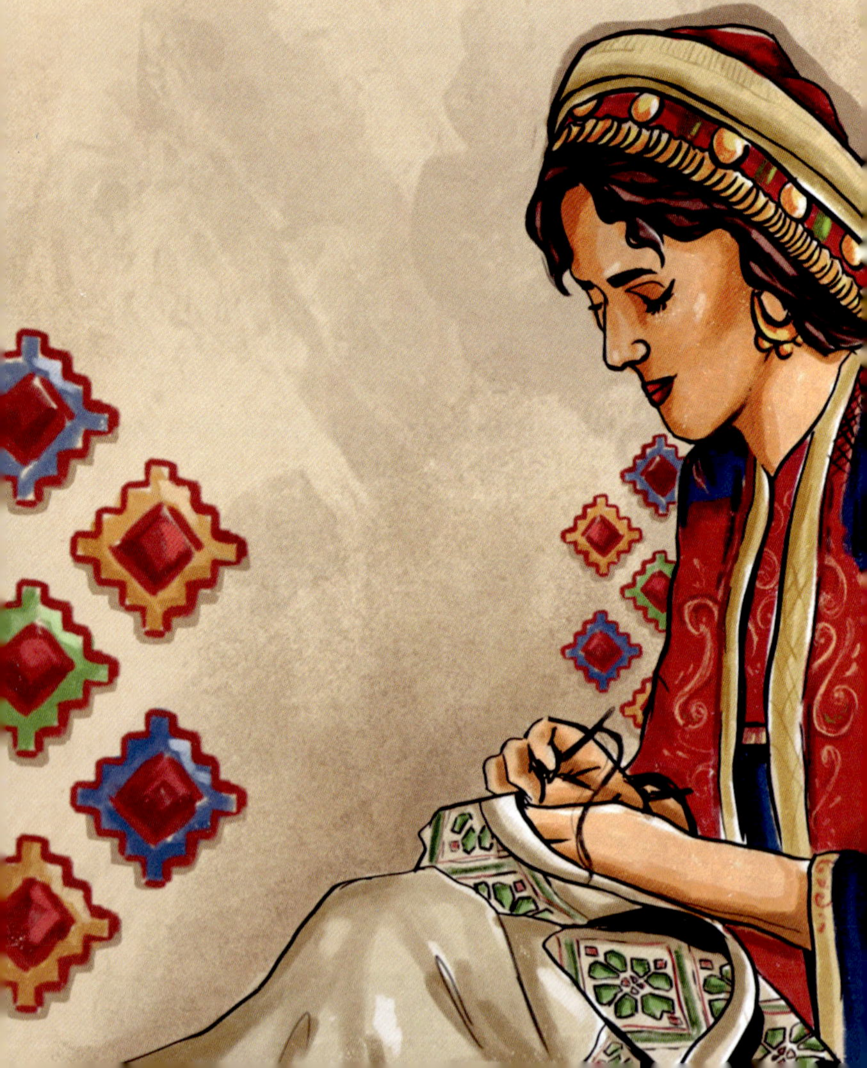

T *for* Tatreez

تَطْرِيز

If you plan to buy a souvenir from Gaza, nothing is better than getting something with Tatreez, the Palestinian embroidery. With needle and thread, stories are told. Tatreez is passed down through generations. The oldest examples date back to the 1840s. This craft was mainly used to embellish the clothing of rural and Bedouin women, including the thobe, abaya, and headcover, with patterns that varied by region. Gazan women are highly skilled in Tatreez drawing inspiration for their designs, decorations, and colours from their natural surroundings and local environment.

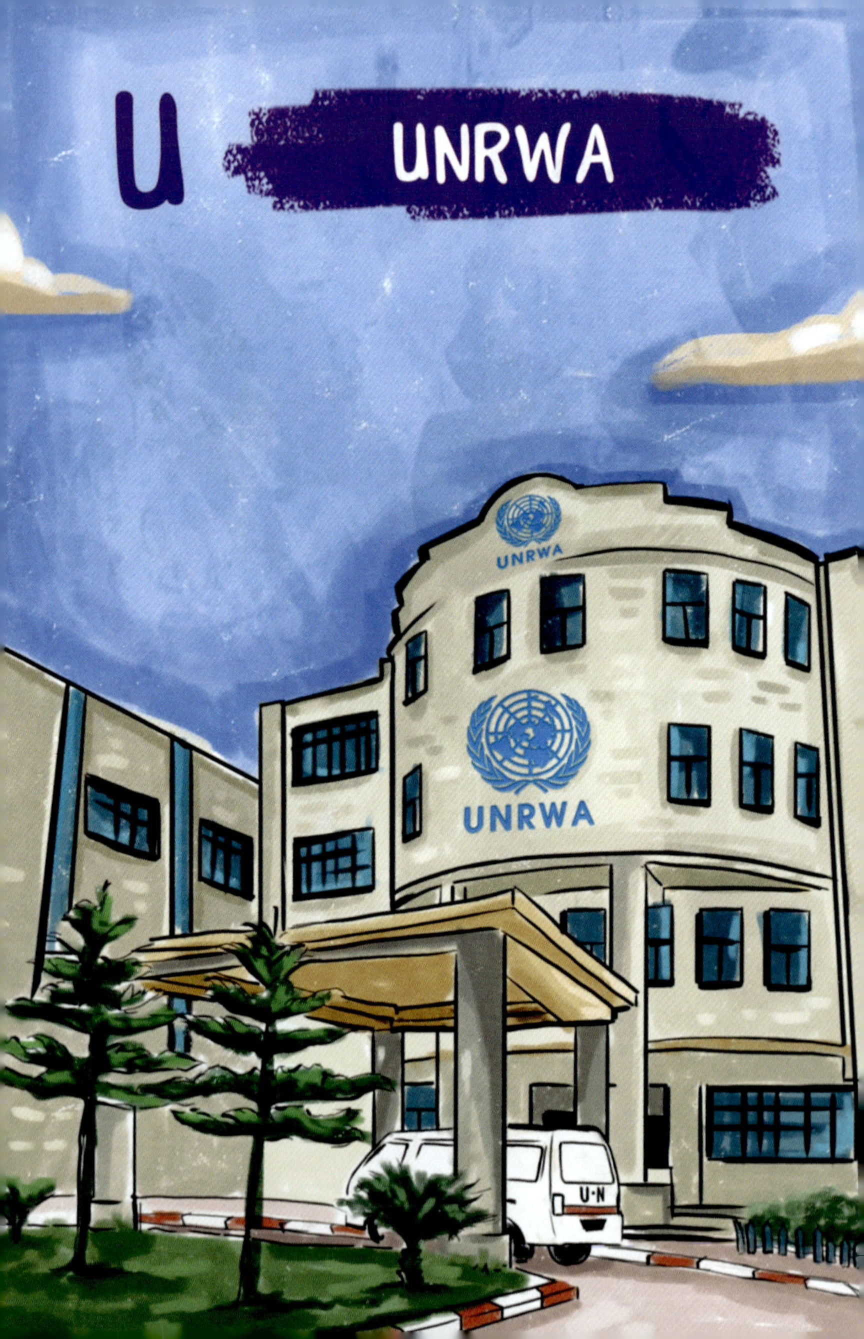
U
UNRWA
UNRWA
UNRWA
U·N

U *for* UNRWA

الأُونْرَوَا

I assure you that in almost every neighbourhood in the Gaza Strip, you will see an UNRWA building. Their distinctive sky-blue buildings are easily recognisable. The United Nations Relief and Works Agency, known locally as Al-Wakala, was established in 1949 after the Israeli occupation of Palestine. UNRWA provides essential services to Palestinian refugees across Jordan, Lebanon, Syria, and the occupied Palestinian territories, including Gaza. The agency operates schools, health clinics, and food distribution centres, playing a vital role in the lives of residents. Many Gazans aspire to work for Al-Wakala due to the job security and the competitive salaries it offers.

V Victory Sign

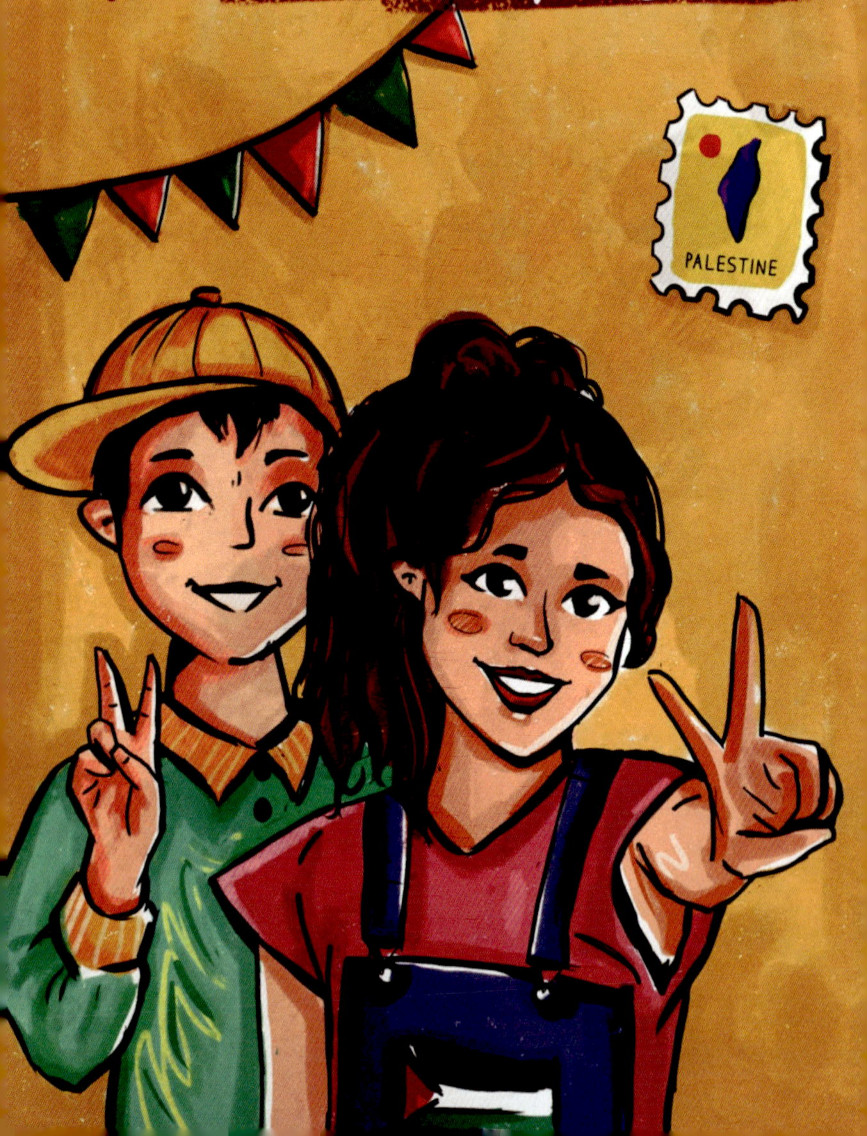

V *for* Victory Sign

عَلَامة النَّصْر

If you take a selfie with Gazans, you'll immediately notice them raising the victory sign! Two fingers raised in a simple V, representing hope and victory. For Palestinians, it has become a powerful symbol in our struggle for freedom. From young to old across the land, this gesture captures our resilience and spirit. It reminds us that despite the challenges, we continue to stand strong and united. Around the world, this symbol, along with the kuffiya, signifies solidarity with Palestine.

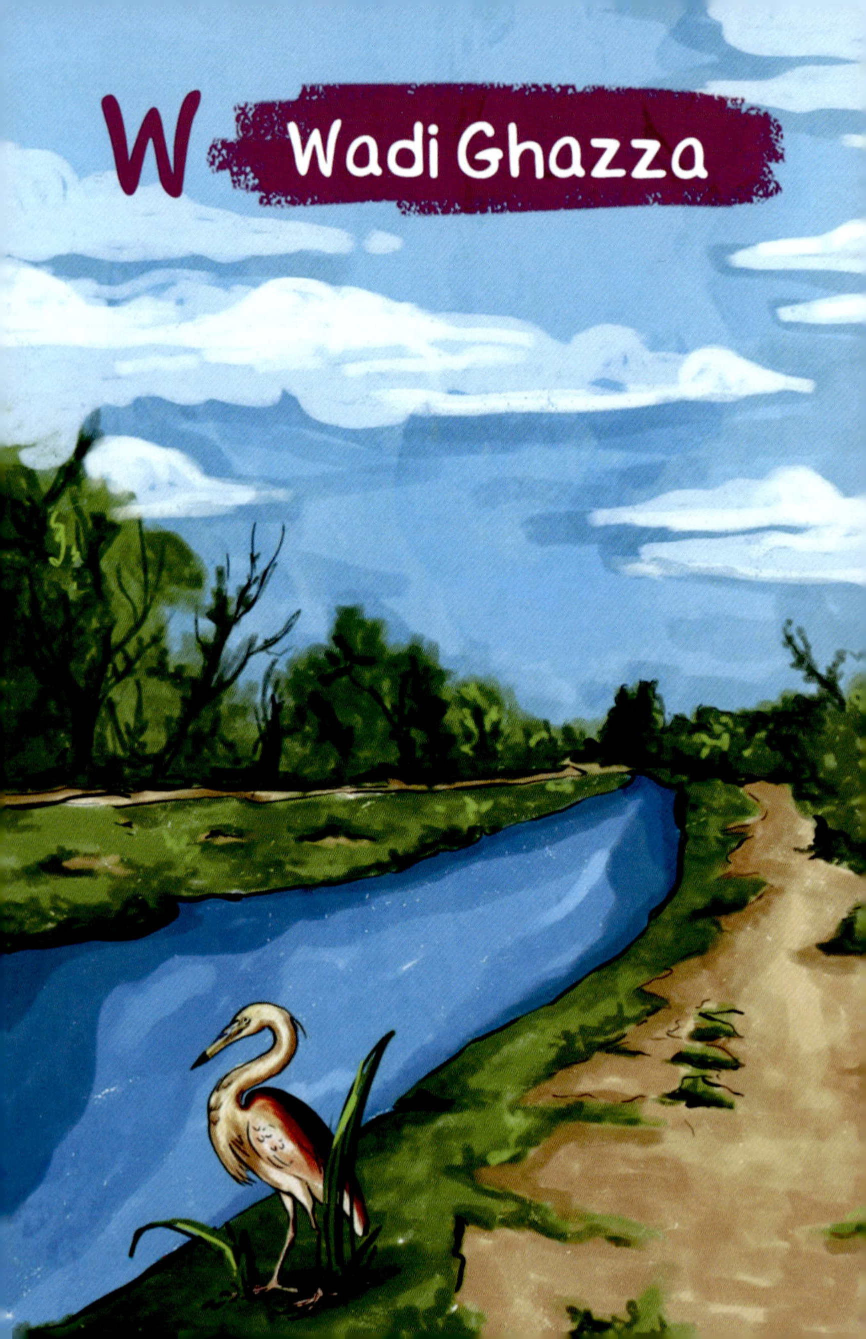
W
Wadi Ghazza

W *for* Wadi Ghazza

وَادِي غَـزَّة

Considered one of the few remaining natural habitats in the Gaza Strip, Wadi Ghazza is worth a visit. This stream or riverbed is located in southern occupied Palestine. It begins in the northern Negev, flows through the Hebron mountains, stretches for 105 kilometers, and empties into the Mediterranean Sea near the city of Zahra, south of Gaza City. Wadi Ghazza has a rich history and has been regarded as a nature reserve and a vital stop for migratory waterbirds like herons, ibises, and quails. The area is also scenic, with various trees and shrubs.

X Xenodochy

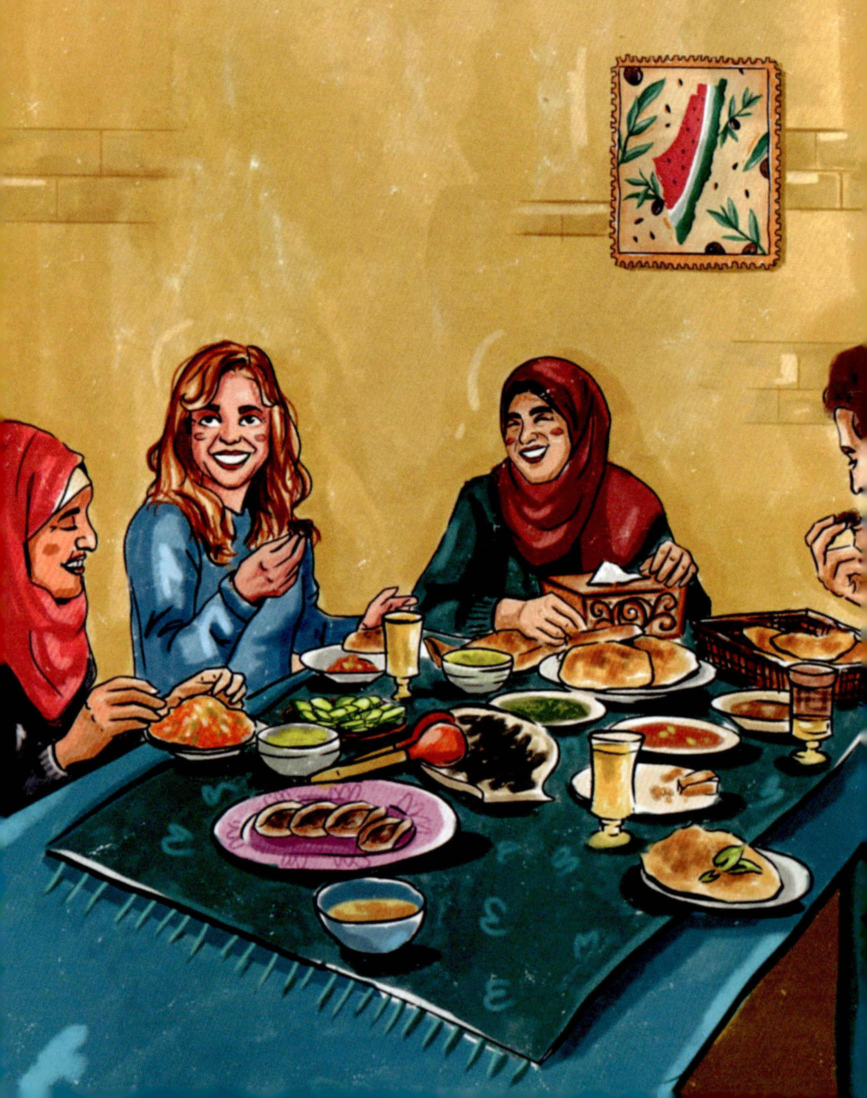

X *for* Xenodochy
حُسْنُ الضِّيَافَة

Let's admit it, there are very few words starting with "X" relevant to Gaza, but this one perfectly captures our welcoming culture. Xenodochy is the art of hospitality and welcoming strangers. As you'll notice when visiting, it's deeply embedded in the cultural fabric of Gaza. Despite everything Gaza has endured, its people shine as exemplars of warmth and generosity. Here, hospitality transcends mere custom; it is a sacred duty and a profound expression of human solidarity. Even with scarce resources, Gazans warmly welcome visitors into their homes, offering hearty meals, sweet tea, and sincere conversation. This tradition of xenodochy exemplifies their resilience and symbolises hope, demonstrating that even in the most challenging circumstances, the spirit of kindness and community prevails. The time when the world will have the chance to visit Gaza and experience our hospitality isn't far. Stay tuned.

Y Al-Yarmouk Stadium

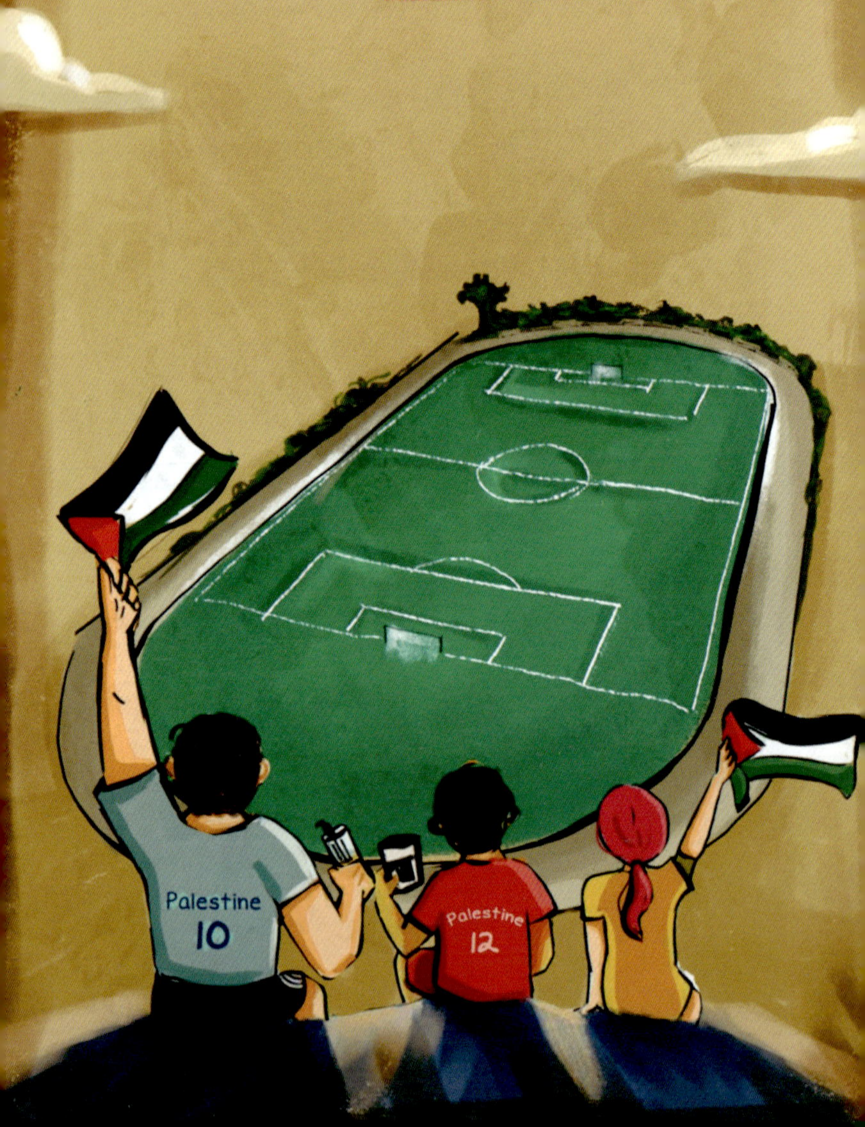

Y *for* Al-Yarmouk Stadium

مَلْعَبُ اليَرْمُوك

If you feel the urge to play football or go for a run while in Gaza, Al-Yarmouk Stadium is the place to be. It's one of the most important sports venues in the Gaza Strip, opened in 1953 during the Egyptian administration. Did you know that over the past 70 years, the stadium has hosted many renowned Arab football clubs, including Egypt's Al-Ahly and several Jordanian teams? In 2010, the stadium hosted the Gaza World Football matches, a symbolic tournament that captured international solidarity with the local football community. Beyond sports, the stadium is also used for large events such as mass weddings and national festivals. Make sure to see a match there; the atmosphere is incredible and a great way to experience local culture.

Z Zawya Market

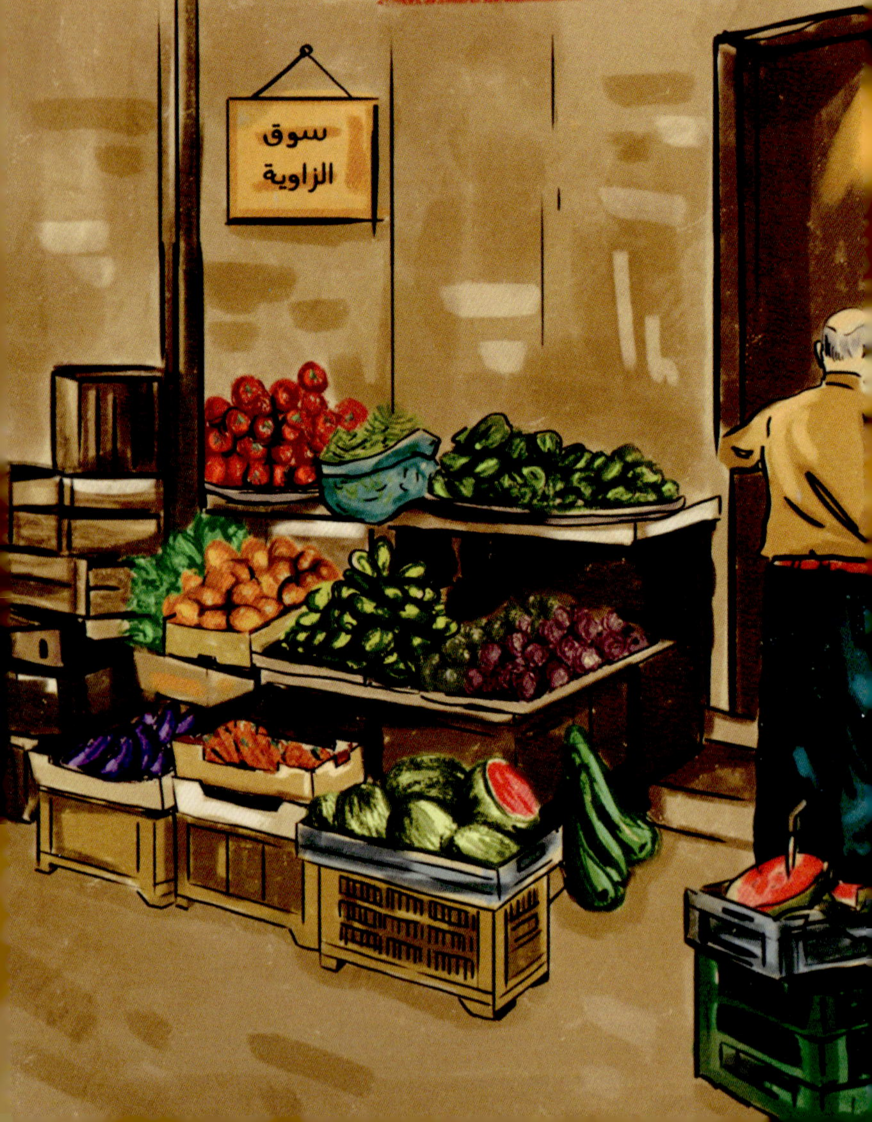

Z for Zawya Market

سُوقُ الزَّاوِيَة

Do you fancy buying some spices and herbs? Zawiya Market is the perfect destination. It's a traditional heritage market located in the heart of the Old Town of Gaza City, between Omar Al-Mukhtar and Al-Wehda streets. A century-old hub beneath Gaza's skies, the market got its name from Indian Muslim traders who bought land to establish a meeting and prayer place known as the Indian Corner (Zawya). There are small shops with narrow doors, offering everything from gold and silver jewellery to various food products and household supplies. The market can get pretty crowded, so be prepared for that. And don't be shy to bargain; it's part of the shopping experience here.

Snippets of what remained

Much of what you read about Gaza in the previous pages has changed forever.

Al-Shifa Hospital has been nearly obliterated; its grounds transformed into mass graves. **Barqouq Castle**, which initially sheltered displaced people in Khan Younis, was bombed and destroyed. **Cinema Al-Samer** met a similar fate.

Despite these calamities, the people of Gaza still strive to find moments of joy, with the Palestinian **Dabkeh** bringing youth and children together.

El-Mina has been decimated, but the city's residents continue to visit, sitting by the crashing waves, hoping for a glimmer of hope.

Fehmi Bek Street's simplicity was destroyed; its tight-knit shops demolished, leaving it in ruins. The "**Gaza Welcomes You" sign** has vanished, but Gaza continues to welcome its loving and supportive visitors.

The sacredness of the **Hashim Mosque** did not protect it from destruction; it suffered the same fate as much of Gaza. The **Islamic University of Gaza**, once the second home to tens of thousands of students, now lies in ruins, its buildings destroyed, and its libraries burned.

Al-Jondi Al-Majhoul Monument truly became unknown, disappearing completely after Omar Al-Mukhtar Street was heavily bulldozed. Some mothers make **Knafah** with whatever ingredients they could find using primitive methods, simply to bring joy to their children's hearts.

Louz season came and went, but the people of Gaza could not taste it as the Louz trees were uprooted, and the agricultural lands bulldozed. Making **Maqloubeh** is difficult now in Gaza, but it remains a Palestinian symbol that has travelled to all continents, causing headaches for unjust policymakers.

Gazans used to eat **Namoura** during happy occasions, but today there is little joy to share this sweet treat with relatives and neighbours. The **Omari Mosque** had its mihrab destroyed and its arcades bombed, but its minaret still stands tall, recording history for future generations.

Church of Saint Porphyrius, like other places of worship in Gaza, was bombed, and some displaced people were killed there. Still, it remains to tell the world that Palestine is a land of religions and acceptance. The rich history within the walls of **Qasr Al-Pasha** vanished under the war machine, leaving only pictures and memories.

The **Rashad El Shawa Centre** no longer exists; it will no longer host cultural, social, and political events because the occupier decided to bomb and destroy it. The fate of **Al-Samrah Bath** is no different; it was destroyed and levelled to the ground.

In tents that offer no protection from the summer heat or winter cold, some Gazan women try to earn their livelihood through **Tatreez**. **UNRWA** is no longer internationally immune; the UN agency has become a target for the occupier, killing hundreds of its employees, and bombing dozens of its schools, shelters, and medicine stores.

The **Victory sign** remains; it is raised by the young and old, the healthy and the wounded, as the occupier will not achieve its goal of crushing the Palestinian will for freedom and dignity. **Wadi Ghazza** has become a defining feature, its north separated from its south, itself a zone of killing and assassination. The birds and animals either shared in the Gazan's death or chose to migrate to safer lands.

They die of hunger, they die of killing, they die of disease, but Gazans remain a symbol of **Xenodochy**, a trait that neither death bombs nor hunger sieges can take away.

Al-Yarmouk Stadium, once a historical venue, became a detention and torture centre for Gazans before the occupier left and completely destroyed it. Finally, **Zawya Market** is no longer the bustling marketplace visited by generations; the war machine turned it into abandoned shops and destroyed alleys.